This
David Bennett Book
belongs to

_____ _____

_____

_____

_____

_____

First published in paperback in 1993
by David Bennett Books Ltd,
94 Victoria Street, St Albans,
Herts, AL1 3TG.
First published in hardback in 1991
by Kingfisher Books

Consultant: Dr Julian Hector

BRITISH LIBRARY CATALOGUING IN PUBLICATION DATA
A catalogue record for this book is available
from the British Library.
ISBN 1 85602 051 7

Typesetting by Type City
Production by Imago
Printed in Hong Kong

I am a Frog

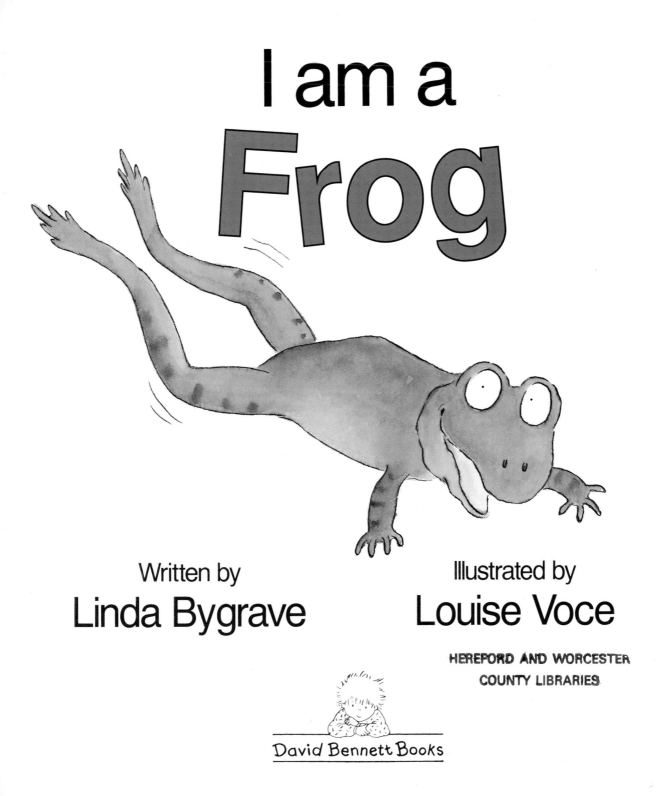

Written by
Linda Bygrave

Illustrated by
Louise Voce

David Bennett Books

I am a frog.
When I sit down ...
I look like this.

When I leap into the air ...
I look like this.

I am green and slimy
and I have to live near water -
usually ponds and streams.

I am a great swimmer because
my feet are webbed. That means
I have skin between my toes.

My long back legs are strong.
I can jump really high!
I have five toes on each of my back feet ...

but only four toes on each front foot.
I don't have a tail, but I did when
I was a baby.

I have big eyes on the top
of my head.
I don't have eyelids like you.

But when I am swimming,
a special skin covers my eyes
to keep out the water.

On land, I breathe the same way
you do. I use my lungs
to breathe air in and out.

But I can do something you can't.
I can breathe underwater.
I breathe through my slimy skin.

I like to eat small slugs and snails.
If I can't find those, I eat
caterpillars and woodlice.

Sometimes I like to catch
a nice, fat, juicy worm.

I gulp at insects
that come too close
to my mouth.

I have a great, big, wide mouth,
but no teeth. So I just swallow
my food whole. Yum-yum!

I have my babies in the spring.
Lots of us gather together and
at night the mummy frogs lay eggs.

Each mummy frog lays about two thousand eggs covered in a clear jelly. This jelly makes the eggs float.

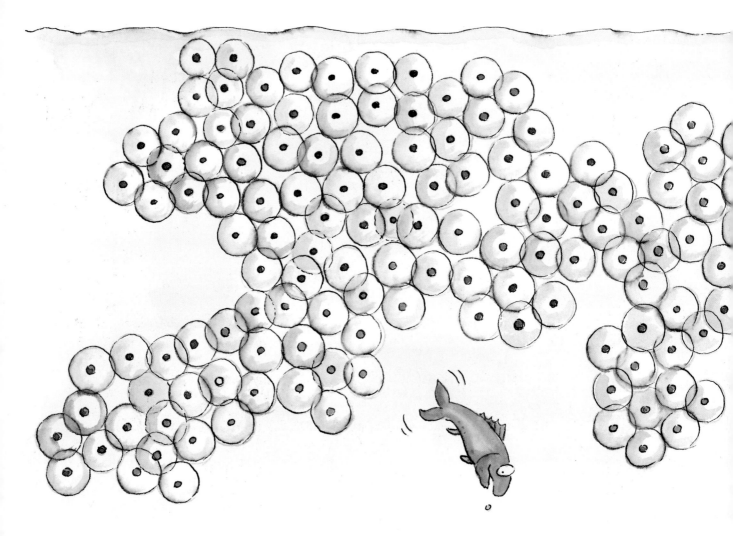

The eggs in the jelly are called
frogspawn. There is lots
and lots of it in ponds in spring.

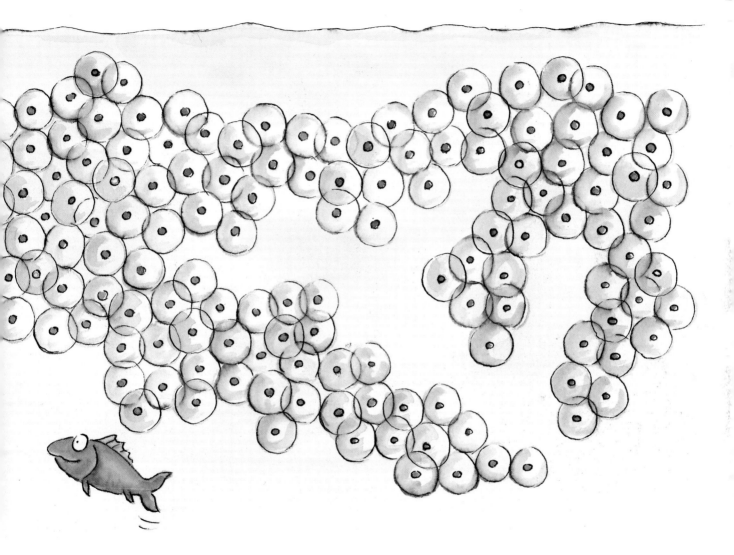

The jelly protects the eggs
from enemies and the cold.
It breaks apart after about two weeks.

The eggs turn into tiny tadpoles.
That is the name for baby frogs.
The tadpoles wriggle out of the jelly.

They don't look like grown-up frogs,
do they? They are small, very dark
and have tails.

After about eight weeks
the tadpoles grow back legs.
They still have a very long tail.

When they are three months old
little front legs appear. And look ...
their tails have become much shorter.

Soon they have wide mouths just like me.
But they are only froglets.
They won't be as big as me for ages.

When they are about three years old,
perhaps they will have babies of their
own. I'm off for a swim. Goodbye!

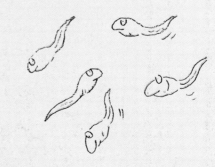

Other David Bennett paperbacks you will enjoy . . .

I am a Duck *Linda Bygrave • Louise Voce* ISBN 1 85602 054 1

I am a Frog *Linda Bygrave • Louise Voce* ISBN 1 85602 051 7

I am a Butterfly *Linda Bygrave • Louise Voce* ISBN 1 85602 052 5

I am a Rabbit *Linda Bygrave • Louise Voce* ISBN 1 85602 053 3

As featured on BBC TV's *Playdays*. The perfect nature library for the very young.

If Dinosaurs Came To Town *Dom Mansell* ISBN 1 85602 044 4

'. . . combines detailed pictures and evocative language with inviting tit-bits of science' *The Independent*

The Monster Book of ABC Sounds *Alan Snow* ISBN 1 85602 041 X

An ABC of sounds, which follows a riotous game of hide-and-seek between a group of rats and monsters.

Inside Big Machines *Arlene Blanchard • Tony Wells* ISBN 1 85602 043 6

A fascinating look inside some of the world's biggest machines.

Teddy Bear, Teddy Bear *Carol Lawson* ISBN 1 85602 040 1

A beautifully illustrated version of the classic children's activity rhyme.

One Cow Moo Moo! *David Bennett • Andy Cooke* ISBN 1 85602 042 8

As featured on BBC TV's *Over The Moon*. A farmyard romp through numbers from one to ten.